HOLT

Civics in Practice
Principles of Government and Economics

HOLT, RINEHART AND WINSTON

A Harcourt Education Company

Orlando • **Austin** • New York • San Diego • London

Copyright © by Holt, Rinehart and Winston

All rights reserved. No part of this publication may be reproduced or transmitted in any form or by any means, electronic or mechanical, including photocopy, recording, or any information storage and retrieval system, without permission in writing from the publisher.

Teachers using CIVICS IN PRACTICE may photocopy complete pages in sufficient quantities for classroom use only and not for resale.

HOLT and the **"Owl Design"** are trademarks licensed to Holt, Rinehart and Winston, registered in the United States of America and/or other jurisdictions.

Printed in the United States of America

If you have received these materials as examination copies free of charge, Holt, Rinehart and Winston retains title to the materials and they may not be resold. Resale of examination copies is strictly prohibited and is illegal.

Possession of this publication in print format does not entitle users to convert this publication, or any portion of it, into electronic format.

ISBN 0-03-077996-0

5 6 7 8 9   912   11 10 9 8 7

Contents

Creative Teaching Strategies

TO THE TEACHER iv

CHAPTER 1   We the People
Collage 1

CHAPTER 2   Foundations of Government
Quick Survey 2

CHAPTER 3   The U.S. Constitution
Ranking 3

CHAPTER 4   Rights and Responsibilities
Resource Speaker 5

CHAPTER 5   The Legislative Branch
Open-Ended Statements 7

CHAPTER 6   The Executive Branch
Role-playing 8

CHAPTER 7   The Judicial Branch
Music, Poetry, and Law 9

CHAPTER 8   State Government
Learning Stations 10

CHAPTER 9   Local Government
Webbing 13

CHAPTER 10   Electing Leaders
Quick Survey 16

CHAPTER 11   The Political System
Interpreting Political Cartoons 17

CHAPTER 12   Paying for Government
Brainstorming 18

CHAPTER 13   Citizenship and the Family
Structured Discussion 20

CHAPTER 14   Citizenship in School
Poetic Expressions 21

CHAPTER 15   Citizenship in the Community
Open-Ended Statements 23

CHAPTER 16   Citizenship and the Law
Continuum 24

CHAPTER 17   The Economic System
Decision Tree 25

CHAPTER 18   Goods and Services
Editorial Page 28

CHAPTER 19   Personal Finances
Webbing 29

CHAPTER 20   Economic Challenges
Brainstorming 32

CHAPTER 21   The U.S. Economy and the World
Open-Ended Statements 34

CHAPTER 22   Career Choices
Ranking 35

CHAPTER 23   Foreign Policy
Predicting Consequences 37

CHAPTER 24   Charting a Course
Issue Strip 38

Each chapter of the student's edition has a creative teaching strategy that corresponds to a teaching objective identified in the Annotated Teacher's Edition. The creative teaching strategies provide you with suggestions for lesson extensions that can be used to stimulate discussion, meet the varied learning styles of students, and actively involve students in the learning process. These strategies are designed for use with the student's edition; however, you may use and adapt them as needed to fit specific classroom settings.

Collage

PURPOSE

In making a collage, students are able to use their imaginations to select visuals depicting attitudes, events, ideas, and individuals connected to a particular topic or time period.

IMPLEMENTATION

1. Prior to this activity, collect magazines, newspapers, and similar materials that can be cut up for use in collages. Select student volunteers to help you prepare and organize the collage materials.

2. Organize the class into several small groups of two to four students each.

3. Assign a chapter-related topic to each group. Select topics from the list below, or develop your own topic list.

   - American Values
   - Responsibilities of Citizenship
   - Qualities of a Good Citizen
   - Immigration Policy
   - Becoming a U.S. Citizen
   - Americans Are from Everywhere
   - A Population on the Move
   - Population Changes
   - Population Growth

4. Encourage students to conduct research and gather more information on their assigned topics.

5. Provide each group with poster board, glue, markers, scissors, and other art materials needed to complete the activity.

6. Decide on a process for giving groups access to the collage materials.

7. Direct group members to work together to select and arrange materials on the poster board. Let the groups know that their collages will be presented to the class without titles or an explanation. Stress that groups need to make their collages clear visual representations of their ideas. Mention that if students have difficulty finding suitable illustrations among the collage materials, they should create their own artwork.

8. Have groups take turns presenting their collages. Ask each collage is presented, have students to list their reactions to the content and the choice of materials used. Record responses on the chalkboard or an easel pad. If students have difficulty understanding what the group was trying to illustrate, ask for suggestions on how the collage could be changed to reflect the group's ideas.

9. Encourage members of each group to comment on the critique of their collage.

10. Display collages around the classroom and use them as a starting point for discussions on various issues related to the chapter "We the People."

Quick Survey

PURPOSE

This strategy allows the teacher and students to observe the range of attitudes and positions held within the class by eliciting opinions on stated issues.

IMPLEMENTATION

1. Make a list of statements that express an opinion on a topic from the chapter or use the statements listed at the end of this strategy.

2. Inform students that you will read a series of statements, and that they must express a position—strongly agree, agree, no opinion, disagree, or strongly disagree—on each one. Give each position a distinct visual signal—raising both hands in the air to indicate strongly agree, thumbs down to indicate strongly disagree, and so on.

3. Make the first statement, allowing students a few moments to think before voting. Record the votes, then move on to the next statement.

4. When you have finished the survey, discuss the various positions with students.

Possible Statements to Survey

- Without government a society cannot function efficiently.

- A representative democracy is a more effective form of government than a direct democracy.

- Absolute monarchies and dictatorships are similar forms of government.

- The only role of the U.S. government is to protect the rights of its people.

- The Declaration of Independence is the most important document in American history.

- The 13 states were justified in wanting to limit the power of the national government under the Articles of Confederation.

- The government that was formed under the Articles of Confederation could never have been a strong government.

- Delegates to the Constitutional Convention relied too much on British sources to create their new government.

- The delegates to the Constitutional Convention should have conducted their meetings publicly.

- The adoption of the Great Compromise demonstrated that the 13 states were ready to become one country.

- The Constitution gave too much power to the federal government.

- Antifederalist arguments against the Constitution were unfounded.

- The Constitution created a strong country by balancing power between the 13 states and the national government.

- The Constitution should not have been implemented without ratification by all 13 states.

Ranking

PURPOSE

This strategy gives students practice in choosing among possible alternatives and in openly defending their choices.

IMPLEMENTATION

1. Decide if you want to undertake this strategy as a class or group activity.

2. Begin by directing students to view the six goals of the Constitution, which are listed on page 88 of the student's edition.

3. Ask students to suggest which goals they consider the most important. As students respond, ask them to explain and justify their choices.

4. Inform students that they are going to vote by a show of hands for the most important of the Constitution's six goals. Read out the statements in the Preamble one at a time, and have students cast their votes after each statement is read. Remind students that they may vote for only one statement. Keep a tally of the votes and record the results on the chalkboard.

5. Next, introduce the idea of weighted tallies. Have students select what they consider the three most important of the Constitution's six goals. Encourage students to explain their selections. Keep score of first-, second-, and third-place votes on a tally sheet similar to the one on the next page. (If you undertake this strategy as a group activity, make a copy of the tally sheet for each group.)

6. Tally the weighted responses by totaling the first-, second-, and third-place votes for each goal. Multiply votes for first place by three, second place by two, and third place by one. Add up the scores for each goal and list the statements on the chalkboard in rank order from top to bottom, with the statement with the highest score at the top.

7. Have students compare the weighted ranking with the original ranking.

TALLY SHEET (Example)

Goals of the Constitution	1st	2nd	3rd	Total
1. Form a more perfect union	4	2	5	21
2. Establish justice	1	0	4	7
3. Ensure domestic tranquillity	0	0	1	1
4. Provide for the common defense	3	1	2	13
5. Promote the general welfare	4	4	1	21
6. Secure the blessings of liberty	5	3	1	22

CHAPTER 3   The U.S. Constitution

TALLY SHEET				
Goals of the Constitution	**1st**	**2nd**	**3rd**	**Total**
1. Form a more perfect union	(___ x 3)	(___ x 2)	(___ x 1)	_________
2. Establish justice	(___ x 3)	(___ x 2)	(___ x 1)	_________
3. Ensure domestic tranquillity	(___ x 3)	(___ x 2)	(___ x 1)	_________
4. Provide for the common defense	(___ x 3)	(___ x 2)	(___ x 1)	_________
5. Promote the general welfare	(___ x 3)	(___ x 2)	(___ x 1)	_________
6. Secure the blessings of liberty	(___ x 3)	(___ x 2)	(___ x 1)	_________

Resource Speaker

PURPOSE

This strategy provides students with an opportunity for face-to-face contact with people who can give authoritative information about the subject under study.

IMPLEMENTATION

1. Begin by checking your school's or district's policy regarding outside speakers.

2. Obtain lists of available speakers in your area. Here are some suggestions for speakers who can talk about the Bill of Rights, civil rights, and the duties and responsibilities of citizenship.

   - Professor of constitutional law

   - Lawyer specializing in constitutional law

   - Member or members from groups such as the American Civil Liberties Union (ACLU), American Federation of Labor and Congress of Industrial Organizations (AFL-CIO), National Association for the Advancement of Colored People (NAACP), National Organization of Women (NOW), or League of United Latin American Citizens (LULAC)

   - Defense attorney or trial lawyer

   - Professor of government or political science who specializes in civil rights

   - Member of your state legislature

   - Professor of women's studies who specializes in the study of women's rights or suffrage

   - Professor of African American, Asian American, American Indian, or Latin American studies who specializes in the study of civil rights

3. Explain to the speaker the goals for the visit, the makeup of your class, and the students' level of understanding of the speaker's area of expertise.

4. Identify topics you wish the speaker to address and discuss the ways he or she will present the information—as audiovisual materials, with class participation, as a lecture, and so on.

5. Explain to students the reason for the speaker's visit, the topics he or she will cover, and the kinds of questions they should be prepared to ask.

6. Encourage students to take notes during the speaker's presentation. These notes may be used for a follow-up exercise in which the students prepare a K-W-L chart similar to the one on the next page. You might use the charts as the basis for a class discussion on the Bill of Rights, civil rights, and the duties and responsibilities of citizenship.

CHAPTER 4   **Rights and Responsibilities**

Specific Topic	What I Knew	What I Wanted to Know	What I Learned

Open-Ended Statements

PURPOSE

This strategy may be used as an introductory activity or as an evaluation tool. As an introductory activity, it provides students with an opportunity to anticipate what they will read. As an evaluation tool, it serves as an alternative to giving a test.

IMPLEMENTATION

1. Begin by writing 8 to 10 sentences that describe important developments, events, or ideas discussed in the chapter. Then list the sentence openings, or sentence stems. These are open-ended statements that students will complete with as many endings as they can. Possible open-ended statements for Chapter 5 include:

- The composition of each house of Congress
- The selection of members of Congress
- The role of committees
- The organization of Congress
- The responsibilities of Congress
- The importance of the elastic clause
- The special powers of Congress
- The limited powers of Congress
- The process of a bill becoming a law
- The benefits of the legislative process

2. If you use this strategy as an introductory activity, use the following guidelines:

- Tell students that you will give them a list of unfinished sentences. Their task is to write as many different endings to the sentences as they can. Point out that this activity is designed to prepare them for reading this chapter.

- When students finish the task, collect their work or have them file it for later use.

- When students finish reading the chapter, use their preliminary work as the basis for what they have learned. Have them view what they wrote as a prediction and compare it to what they now know.

3. If you use this strategy as an evaluation tool, use the following guidelines:

- Prepare a list of sentence endings based on material in the chapter. Use this as a measure of students' understanding of the chapter.

- List the sentence stems on the chalkboard and tell students to complete each sentence in as many ways as the chapter content provides endings.

- Have students skim the chapter to find the appropriate information or have them write from memory.

- Encourage students to share and compare their completed sentences.

Role Playing

PURPOSE

Role playing allows students to assume the persona of someone they are studying. This strategy engages students in the subject matter in an entertaining way. It also allows for a creative avenue through which students can demonstrate their understanding.

IMPLEMENTATION

1. Role playing can be done while you are teaching a chapter or as a review prior to a test. Assigning students the roles of individuals they are studying helps them to review the chapter's main ideas.

2. Organize students into pairs or small groups, assigning each pair or group one of the topics listed at the end of the strategy. Alternatively, assign topics of your own choosing.

3. Direct students to study the individuals involved in their assigned topic. Whether students play famous people or ordinary individuals, they should attempt to present realistic portrayals.

4. Once they have completed their research, have pairs or groups work together to develop scripts that will serve as the basis for scenarios related to their topics.

5. Next, have pairs or groups rehearse their scenarios. Point out that they do not need to commit their lines to memory, since they will be allowed to use their scripts during the actual performance.

6. Have each pair or group perform its scenario. Before the performances, remind students that they must remain in character throughout.

7. After the performances, have the class discuss the effectiveness of the role-playing. Guide the discussion by asking questions like the following: What were the main points made in each performance? How well did the players in each performance succeed in getting across the information they wanted to communicate? What changes do you think would make the message of each performance clearer?

8. Encourage players to review and comment on the critiques of their performances.

Possible Topics for Role-Playing Scenarios

- A discussion between George Washington and Franklin D. Roosevelt about the advantages and disadvantages of term limits

- The president delivering a State of the Union Address to Congress

- The president negotiating foreign policy with a world leader

- An interview with the president about his or her daily life

- A White House staff meeting

- A meeting between the Department of Defense and the National Security Council

- A press conference with the president's press secretary

- A cabinet meeting

Music, Poetry, and Law

PURPOSE

This strategy encourages students to synthesize their knowledge of a legal or political concept by creating poems or songs.

IMPLEMENTATION

1. Begin by organizing students into groups of three, four, or five.

2. Give each group a copy of the following terms:
   - Authority
   - Appeal
   - Common law
   - Precedent
   - Judiciary Act of 1789
   - John Marshall
   - Jurisdiction
   - Court of appeals
   - The Supreme Court
   - Judicial review
   - *Brown* v. *Board of Education*
   - Voting rights

3. Inform students that their task is to write two poems or songs, each including at least one of the listed terms. Mention that one of the poems or songs should address the responsibilities of the judicial branch, while the other should address the role of the U.S. court system. Also, add that each poem or song should reflect the particular perspective of the writer on the subject matter—praising, mourning, satirizing, or pleading, for example. These feelings should be expressed or implied in the words and structure of the poems or songs.

4. Review some basic directions for writing poems and songs with students. This might include brainstorming and selecting ideas, words, and phrases; organizing ideas; writing a draft; revising; and editing. Offer guidelines for the length of the poems and songs. Poems might run between 8 and 16 lines, while songs could contain from 2 to 4 short verses.

5. Point out that if groups write songs, they should use familiar melodies or make up their own tunes.

6. Provide each group with markers and poster board or butcher paper. Tell students to use these materials to present their poems or songs for display.

7. Have each group read their poems or sing their songs. Encourage students who play musical instruments to accompany the singing performances.

8. If audiovisual equipment is available, you may wish to videotape the performances.

9. Following each performance, encourage student discussion by asking questions such as the following: What was the poem (song) about? What point of view was expressed in the poem (song)? Do you agree or disagree with that point of view?

Learning Stations

PURPOSE

This strategy provides students with the opportunity to learn, synthesize, and evaluate information in an open classroom environment. Although the activity is highly structured, students must be self-directed in their pursuit of information. This strategy works well as a means of disseminating new information or reviewing information that has already been learned.

IMPLEMENTATION

1. Begin by developing a series of tasks related to the chapter. Each task should be an independent activity so that students may undertake the tasks in any order.

2. Set up stations around the classroom with a task at each station. Distribute scorecards to students as a way for them to identify the different perspectives offered at each learning station.

3. Organize students into teams of two or three. Direct teams to go to a vacant station to begin the activity. Point out that each team member should take an active part in completing each task. For example, each student should read and discuss the task signs and take turns making entries on their scorecards.

4. After teams have completed one task, they should move on to another vacant station. If there are no vacant stations, team members should check their work while they wait for an opening.

5. Once all the teams have completed all the tasks, encourage students to share and compare their answers or solutions.

THE SEPARATE AND SHARED CHARACTERISTICS OF THE FEDERAL AND STATE GOVERNMENTS

Teaching Strategy:

1. Construct Learning Station signs and place them at regular intervals around the classroom.

2. Group students into teams of two or three. Provide each team with a copy of the scorecard.

3. Direct teams to go to a vacant station.

4. Tell team members to read and discuss the statement on the sign. Then have them consider whether each statement represents the federal government, state governments, or both.

5. Have one team member enter the Learning Station number in the correct column on the scorecard. Encourage team members to take turns making scorecard entries.

6. Once teams have completed all the Learning Stations, have them share and explain their answers.

7. Complete the activity by leading a class discussion on the role and powers of the federal government versus state governments.

Learning Station Signs:

1. Provides for public safety	**6.** Divided into executive, judicial, and legislative branches
2. Oversees elections	**7.** Maintains school systems
3. Makes and enforces laws	**8.** Accepts the full faith and credit clause
4. Conducts foreign policy	**9.** Has the power to tax its citizens
5. Establishes court systems	**10.** Maintains a military

SCORECARD ANSWERS

State Governments	Federal Government
2.	1.
3.	3.
5.	4.
6.	5.
7.	6.
8.	9.
9.	10.

CHAPTER 8   State Government

SCORECARD

State Governments	Federal Government

Webbing

PURPOSE

This mental mapping strategy encourages students to think critically as they explore the relationships among events, ideas, and people in a reading passage, lesson, or unit. It may also be used as an assessment tool at the end of a section, chapter, or unit.

IMPLEMENTATION

1. Direct students to begin by identifying the main idea, event, or individual from a set reading passage, lesson, or unit.

2. Then provide students with copies of the diagram on the page 15. Have students enter the main idea, event, or individual in the center circle of the diagram.

3. In the outer circles, have students enter information that is connected or related to the main idea, event, or individual. For example, you might ask students to read Section 3 of Chapter 9 and web the information on city government. After entering *City Government* in the center circle, students then might add information to the outer circles about how city governments are established, why city government is needed, and how state and city governments cooperate with each other. See sample diagram on the following page.

4. Have students share and compare their completed webs. Encourage students to explain why they included particular facts about the units of local government.

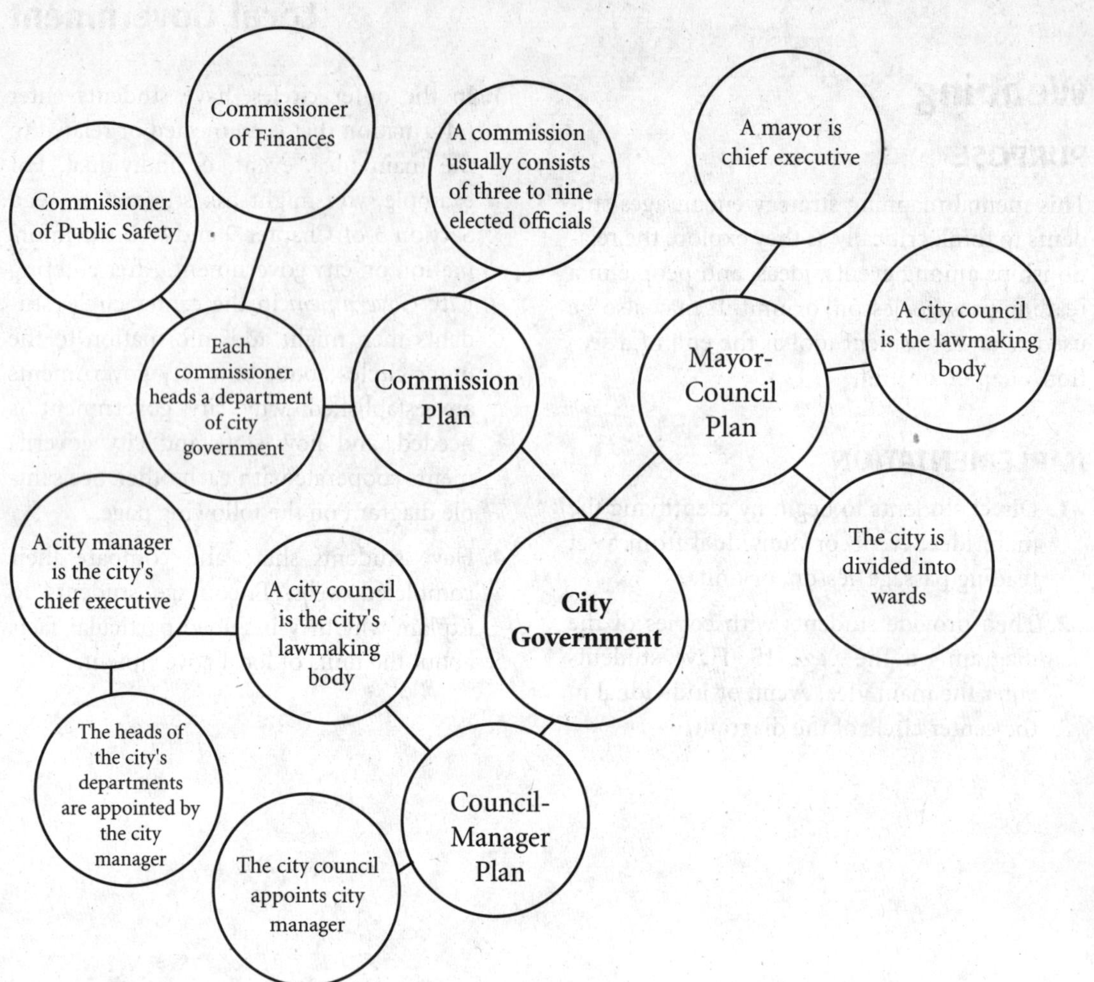

Commissioner of Finances
Commissioner of Public Safety
A commission usually consists of three to nine elected officials
A mayor is chief executive
Each commissioner heads a department of city government
Commission Plan
Mayor-Council Plan
A city council is the lawmaking body
A city manager is the city's chief executive
A city council is the city's lawmaking body
City Government
The city is divided into wards
The heads of the city's departments are appointed by the city manager
The city council appoints city manager
Council-Manager Plan

CHAPTER 9   **Local Government**

Use this web as a starting point. Then add or remove circles and lines as necessary.

Quick Survey

PURPOSE

This strategy allows the teacher and students to observe the range of attitudes and positions held within the class by eliciting opinions on stated issues.

IMPLEMENTATION

1. Make a list of statements that express an opinion on a topic from the chapter or use the statements listed at the end of this strategy.

2. Inform students that you will read a series of statements, and that they must express a position—strongly agree, agree, no opinion, disagree, or strongly disagree—on each one. Give each position a distinct visual signal—raising both hands in the air to indicate strongly agree, thumbs down to indicate strongly disagree, and so on.

3. Read the first statement, allowing students a few moments to think before voting. Record the votes, then move on to the next statement.

Possible Statements to Survey

- Political parties have too much power in government.

- Political parties provide a voice and a means for people with similar ideas to affect government policy.

- Third parties play an insignificant role in a two-party system.

- Political parties are unorganized beyond the national level.

- The requirements set forth in the Federal Election Campaign Act are necessary to control political corruption.

- The spending of public funds in political campaigns should not be regulated.

- The right to vote is the most important right held by American citizens.

- Anyone should be able to vote in the United States.

- Registering to vote is necessary.

- Voting by secret ballot is an effective and fair way for individuals to vote.

- Primary elections are an important part of the political process.

- The electoral college provides an effective method of voting for president.

- The electoral college should be replaced with a system of direct election by popular vote.

Interpreting Political Cartoons

PURPOSE

Cartoons capture students' attention and stimulate their thinking. This strategy provides guidelines for interpreting political cartoons and offers students an opportunity to translate their knowledge into a creative and entertaining medium.

IMPLEMENTATION

1. Begin by displaying several examples of political cartoons. Possible sources include: *Best Editorial Cartoons of the Year* (Pelican, published annually), edited by Charles Brooks; *Drawn & Quartered: The History of American Political Cartoons* (Elliott & Clark, 1996), by Stephen Hess and Sandy Northrop; and *Them Damned Pictures: Explorations in American Political Cartoon Art* (Archon Books, 1996), by Roger A. Fischer.

2. Review with the class the techniques cartoonists use to convey their points of view.

   - Caricature—distorting or exaggerating an individual's physical features

   - Stereotyping—making oversimplified, exaggerated, or unfavorable generalizations about a particular group of people

   - Symbols—using signs or objects to represent ideas

   - Labels—using words to identify elements of the cartoon

   - Exaggeration—portraying an individual or situation as larger than life

   As you detail these techniques, call on students to find examples in the displayed books of cartoons.

3. Have students work in small groups to identify topics discussed in the chapter on which to base cartoons. If groups have difficulty identifying topics, provide them with the following list:

   - Influences on public opinion

   - Propaganda techniques

   - Polling and sampling

   - The role of interest groups

   - The role of citizens in the political process

   - Attitudes of nonvoting citizens

   - Voter turnout

   - Political action committees and political campaigns

   Have group members discuss each topic to clarify the ideas and information they think should be presented in the cartoons. Encourage students to take notes during these discussions.

4. Ask each student to select a topic from the group list. Have students draw a political cartoon about their selected topic using one or more of the cartooning techniques.

5. Call on volunteers to present and discuss their cartoons. Use these presentations as a springboard for a class discussion focusing on how well the cartoons conveyed the issues they addressed. You might also have students compare cartoons that addressed the same issue or that used the same cartooning techniques.

Brainstorming

PURPOSE

The brainstorming process encourages students to use their imagination and creativity to develop different approaches or solutions to a given problem.

IMPLEMENTATION

1. Decide whether you will conduct this strategy as a class activity or group activity.

2. Identify a problem discussed in the chapter, or select one from the following list:

   - The cost of government
   - Prioritizing funding for programs
   - Paying off the national debt
   - The use of property taxes to fund public schools
   - Government borrowing

   - Balancing the federal budget
   - Controlling federal spending
   - Raising revenue to pay for government

3. Write the problem in the center of the board or easel pad and circle it.

4. Ask students to come up with as many solutions to the problem as they can, including those that seem impractical or wild. Do not comment on students' suggestions or open them to discussion. Write and circle suggestions in the area surrounding the circled problems. Draw lines to connect the outer circles to the central circle. When all responses have been noted, encourage students to discuss and accept, reject, or modify the various solutions.

5. Repeat the brainstorming process for other problems. Call on volunteers to write responses on the board or easel pad and to lead discussions of the solutions.

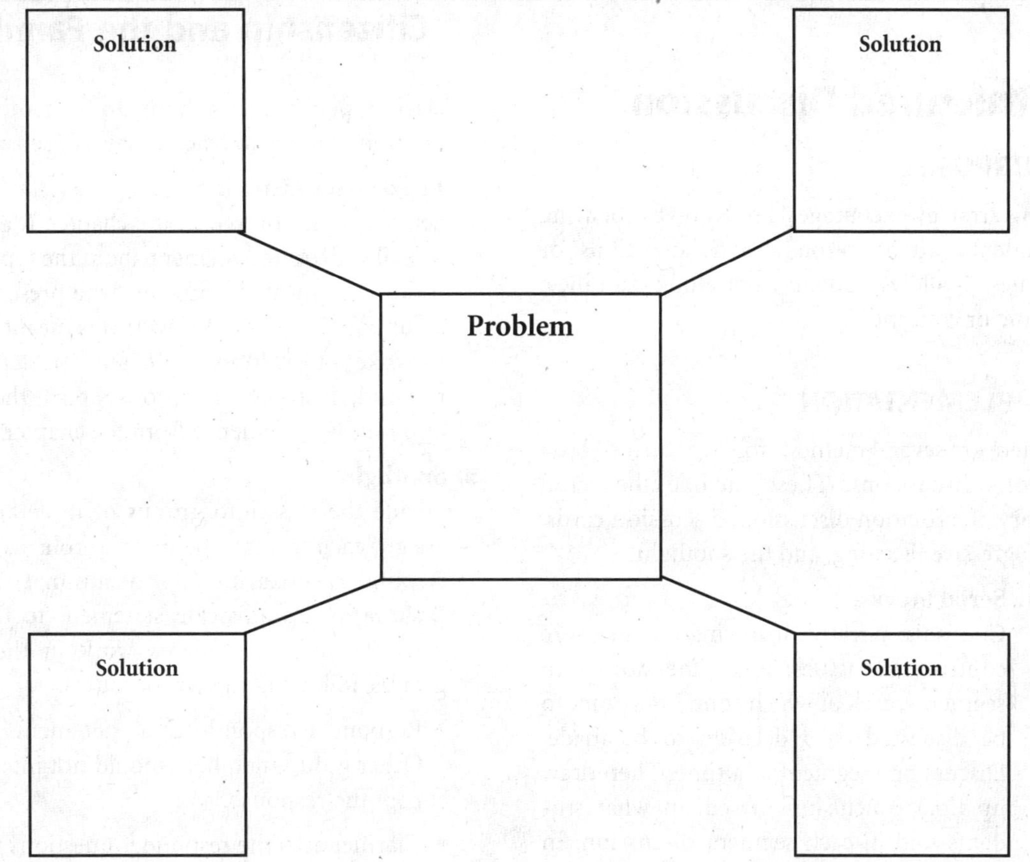

Solution
Solution
Problem
Solution
Solution

Structured Discussion

PURPOSE

This strategy encourages discussion by focusing students' attention on specific questions or issues. It allows students to carefully examine a topic or concept.

IMPLEMENTATION

There are several methods for structuring classroom discussions. These include the serial story, the rotation discussion, discussion cards, progressive listening, and the spotlight.

1. **Serial Story**

   Choose a narrative involving one or more controversial issues. Break the story into segments, each of which contains a point to be discussed or a decision to be made. Discuss one segment at a time. Then draw up final conclusions based on what students said in each segment discussion. In Chapter 13, the serial story approach works particularly well with the discussion of the role and powers of family law.

2. **Rotation Discussion**

   Draw up a list of discussion questions related to the content of Chapter 13 and assign each question a number. Then assign a corresponding number to each student. Select a number and read the question. The student with the corresponding number will be the first to discuss the question. Other students may volunteer their opinions after the first student is finished. This strategy works well in conjunction with the serial story approach.

3. **Discussion Cards**

   Identify a topic from the chapter. Draft discussion questions on the topic and write them on index cards—one question per card. Organize the class into groups of three or four students and give each group a discussion card. Have groups discuss their questions and try to come to a consensus. Then have group representatives present the results of their discussion to the class. Open the questions to dissenting opinions and try to reach a class consensus.

4. **Progressive Listening**

   Select a topic covered in the chapter. Make a devil's advocate statement about the topic. A devil's advocate is someone who presents an unpopular point of view that is meant to provoke a response. When students respond, instruct them to support their opinions with evidence from the chapter.

5. **Spotlight**

   Divide the class into groups of three and assign each group member a role as a responder, a clarifier, or a summarizer. Make a devil's advocate statement to the class. Then have students work in their groups, following these procedures:

   • Responder responds to the statement. Other group members should not interrupt the response.

   • Clarifier asks the responder questions to clarify any points in the response.

   • Summarizer then restates what has taken place, showing how the responder and the clarifier played their roles.

   If time permits, have group members change roles until all students have played responder, clarifier, and summarizer.

Possible Discussion Topics

• Changes in family life since colonial times

• Different types of families

• Effects of the increasing numbers of women in the workforce

• Regulations set forth by marriage laws

• Protection of children's legal rights

• Factors affecting the divorce rate in the United States

• Responsibilities taught within families

• Using compromise to settle disputes

• The purpose of a family budget

Poetic Expressions

PURPOSE

This strategy encourages students to extend their critical thinking abilities by using poetic forms to explore concepts, use terminology, and show an understanding of the important life skills that they learn in school.

IMPLEMENTATION

1. Review with students the three poetic forms discussed below. Assign each student one of these forms or have students select their own.

2. Have students write a poem using their poetic form on a topic related to the chapter content. Students should choose their topics from the lists below or they may come up with their own topics based on Chapter 14.

3. Have students read their poems to the class.

4. Using the guidelines at the end of this activity, lead a constructive discussion and analysis of each poem.

Cinquain

A cinquain is a poem that contains 22 syllables in five lines. Each line has a specific role and a set number of syllables, as shown in the following model.

Line number	Role	Number of syllables	Example
1	title	2	college
2	description	6	higher education
3	action	7	studying for a degree
4	emotions experienced	5	excitement and hope
5	synonym for title	3	career preparation

Diamante

A diamante is a seven-line poem similar to a cinquain. However, instead of using a set number of syllables per line, the object of a diamante is to create a particular shape—roughly like a diamond. Each line has a suggested role, as shown in the following model.

Line	Role	Example
1	Noun or subject	learning
2	Two adjectives	objective, organized
3	Three words ending in -ing	observing, conditioning, participating
4	Four words about the subject	the result of experience
5	Three more -ing words	thinking, analyzing, concentrating
6	Two more adjectives	motivational, insightful
7	Synonym for the subject	discovery

Acrostic

An acrostic is a poem in which the first letter of each line, when arranged vertically, spells out one or more base words. In an acrostic, there is no set rhythm or rhyme scheme; it is written in free verse. However, each line should say something about the base word. In the following model, the base word is *education*.

Encouraging learning and understanding
Develops talents and skills for
Use in your future.
Citizenship taught in school
Aims to provide equal opportunities
Through equal education.
Inviting you to think for yourself
Opinions and ideas may be challenged.
No barriers to fulfilling your dreams.

Here are concepts or topics that students may choose to use as their base word for an acrostic poem:

• Health habits	• Graduate school
• High school	• Mainstreaming
• Organization	• College
• Creativity	• Study skills
• Reasoning	• Insight
• Conditioning	• Prejudice
• Motivation	• Cooperation
• Tutoring	• Citizenship

Discussion and Analysis Guidelines

Analyzing others' poems can help students develop their understanding of a topic and help them with their own writing. After each student reads his or her poem, encourage the rest of the class to review the work based on the following questions:

- Does the writer communicate information in a straightforward manner?
- What aspects of the topic did the writer address?
- Whom does the writer address in his or her poem?
- What is the tone of the writer's voice in the poem?
- What is the writer's point of view?
- Was the writer persuasive in presenting his or her point of view? Why or why not?
- Would you change any of the writer's lines or words? Why or why not?

After students have reviewed all of the poems, encourage them to write another poem in any form. In writing this poem, they should use what they have learned from other students' work.

Open-Ended Statements

PURPOSE

This strategy may be used as an introductory activity or as an evaluation tool. As an introductory activity, it provides students with an opportunity to anticipate what they will read. As an evaluation tool, it serves as an alternative to giving a test.

IMPLEMENTATION

1. Begin by writing 8 to 10 sentences that describe important developments, events, or ideas discussed in the chapter. Then list the sentence openings, or sentence stems. These are open-ended statements that students will complete with as many endings as they can. Possible open-ended statements for Chapter 15 include:

- The purpose of communities
- The establishment of crossroads
- The effects of transportation on urban growth
- The role of climate and resources in the formation of communities
- The difference between small country towns and suburbs
- Meeting challenges in communities
- The work of volunteer groups
- The benefits of community recreation facilities
- The relationship between urban areas and metropolitan areas
- The ability to communicate

2. If you use this strategy as an introductory activity, use the following guidelines:

- Tell students that you will give them a list of unfinished sentences. Their task is to write as many different endings to the sentences as they can. Point out that this activity is designed to prepare them for reading this chapter.
- When students finish the task, collect their work or have them file it for later use.
- When students finish reading the chapter, use their preliminary work as the basis for a discussion of what they have learned. Have them view what they wrote as a prediction and compare it to what they now know.

3. If you use this strategy as an evaluation tool, use the following guidelines:

- Prepare a list of sentence endings based on material in the chapter. Use this as a measure of students' understanding of the chapter.
- List the sentence stems on the chalkboard and tell students to complete each sentence in as many ways as the chapter content provides endings.
- Have students skim the chapter to find the appropriate information or have them write from memory.
- Encourage students to share and compare their completed sentences.

Continuum

PURPOSE

This activity allows students to express and defend positions on given issues. In doing so, students will need to consider arguments and perspectives that differ from their own.

IMPLEMENTATION

1. Begin by directing students to read the paragraphs under the title "The Juvenile Justice System" on textbook page 396. When students have completed the reading, have them consider whether or not they agree with the Supreme Court's ruling that juveniles accused of crimes do not have the right to a trial by jury. To encourage students to think about the subject, ask—but do not take responses to—the following questions: Should juveniles accused of crimes have the same rights to due process as adults accused of crimes? Why might the Supreme Court have decided to rule that juveniles accused of crimes do not have the right to a trial by jury?

2. Clear a wide space in the classroom. Draw an imaginary line across the room and tell students that this line represents a continuum. Inform students that you will ask them a question and they must answer by positioning themselves along the continuum.

3. Ask the following question: Should juveniles accused of committing crimes have the right to a jury trial? Designate one end of the continuum as "right to a trial by jury" and the other end as "no right to a trial by jury." Then tell students that they should stand somewhere on the continuum to indicate their responses to this question. For example, students who strongly believe that juveniles accused of crimes have the right to a jury trial should stand at the "right to a trial by jury" end. Students who strongly believe that juveniles accused of a crime do not have the right to a jury trial should stand at the "no right to a trial by jury" end. Those students who believe that in some cases juveniles accused of crimes may or may not have the right to a jury trial should stand somewhere in the middle.

4. Allow students one or two minutes to take their places on the continuum. Make sure that they accomplish this in an orderly fashion.

5. Ask students at one end of the continuum to explain their reasons for holding this position. Then, ask students at the other end to do the same. Continue asking students at different positions on the continuum until you have a range of views on the issue.

6. Allow students an opportunity to change their positions on the continuum. Ask those who choose to move why they changed their views.

Juveniles' Right to a Trial by Jury

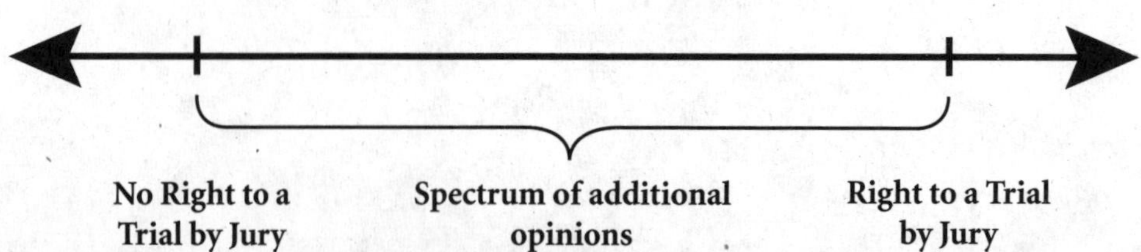

The Economic System

Decision Tree

PURPOSE

This strategy helps students think about possible alternatives and consequences when faced with making a decision. It is particularly useful when students are grappling with large issues or complex circumstances that present no clear-cut or easy solutions.

IMPLEMENTATION

1. Begin by organizing students into groups of two or three.

2. Make copies of the Decision Tree B handout and distribute one to each group.

3. Set the scene for the decision by directing students to imagine that they are entrepreneurs preparing to start their own business. They must decide if they want to establish a sole proprietorship, a partnership, or a corporation.

4. Have a group member enter sole proprietorship, partnership, and corporation along the trunk of the Decision Tree.

5. Have group members take turns entering the positive and negative consequences of each alternative in the foliage of the Decision Tree.

6. Ask group members to discuss all the consequences and then decide which alternative they would choose. Have a group member enter the selection at the top of the Decision Tree.

7. Allow time for groups to share and discuss their decisions.

Decision Tree A may be used for Chapter 17 in the following way:

Ask students to decide if the federal government should become more involved in the regulation of business.

CHAPTER 17 · **The Economic System**

Decision Tree A

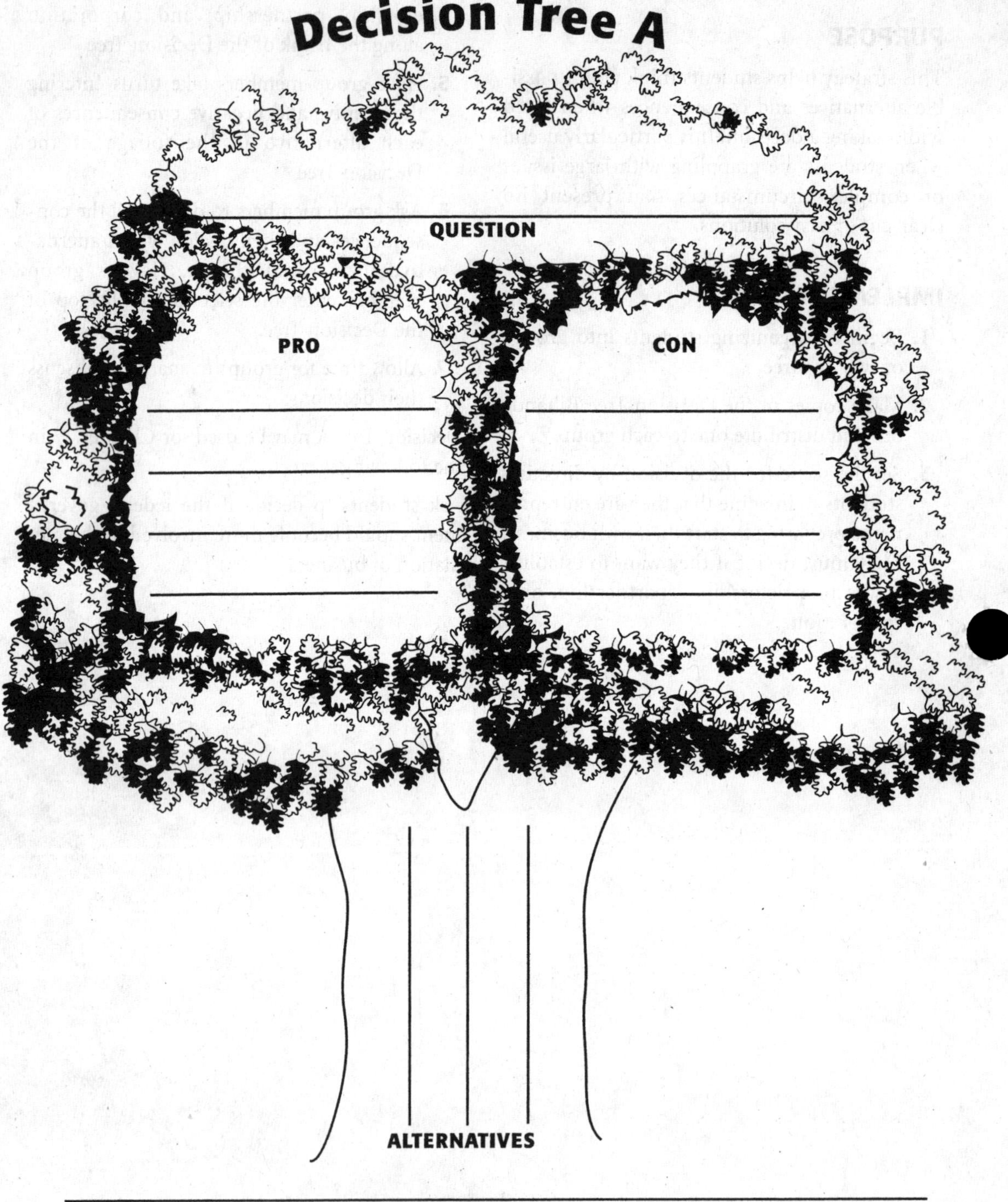

CHAPTER 17   The Economic System

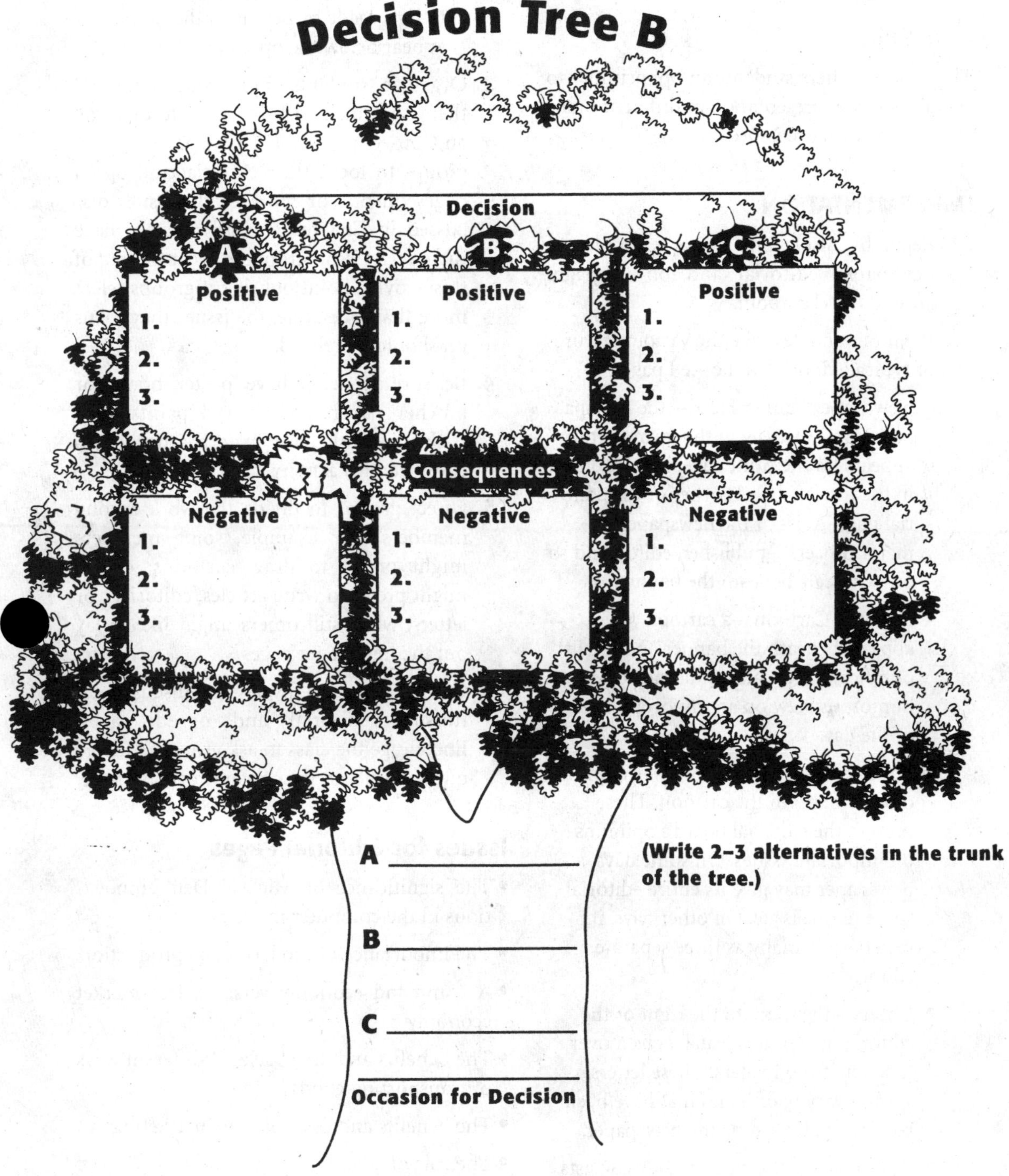

Editorial Page

PURPOSE

This strategy offers students an opportunity to create a visual representation of different opinions on one or more issues.

IMPLEMENTATION

1. Begin by displaying several examples of newspaper editorial and op-ed pages around the classroom.

2. Point out and describe the various features of typical editorial and op-ed pages.

   - Newspaper Banner Head—the newspaper's name, usually in the form that it appears on the front page, is reproduced in the top left-hand corner of the editorial page. A list of the newspaper's major officers—publisher, editor, and so on—appears beneath the banner.

   - Editorial Cartoon—a cartoon often appears beneath the banner and the list of officers. The cartoon usually offers a humorous view on an important issue of the day.

   - Editorials—editorials normally appear directly beneath the cartoon. These present the editorial board's opinions on important issues. On some days, a newspaper may give its entire editorial space to one issue. On other days, it may have as many as three separate editorials.

   - Letters—the space to the right of the editorial material is usually given over to letters from readers. These letters cover a variety of issues that have been recently addressed by the newspaper.

   - Op-ed page—this page usually consists of articles, sometimes written by politicians or other prominent people, expressing opinions on important issues. (You might mention to students that this page gets its name because it appears *op*posite the *ed*itorial page.)

   - Quotations—in some newspapers, quotations made by people in the news appear below the op-ed articles.

3. Organize students into groups and tell them that their task is to create editorial and op-ed pages for a newspaper. Direct groups to focus their editorial and op-ed pages on one or more of the issues discussed in Chapter 18. Alternatively, have them select issues from the list at the end of this activity. Point out that if groups select more than one issue, the issues they focus on should be related.

4. Be sure students have poster board or butcher paper, pencils and paints, glue sticks, and other art materials needed to complete this activity.

5. Direct groups to divide the work among members. For example, some members might prefer to draw cartoons; others might prefer to write articles, editorials, or letters; while still others might like to lay out the newspaper pages.

6. Call on groups to display and discuss their finished editorial and op-ed pages. Encourage the class to ask group members questions about the contents of their page.

Issues for Editorial Pages

- The significance of Michael Dell's innovations in the computer industry
- The importance of modern mass production
- A command economy versus a free-market economy
- The benefits and drawbacks of different ways of transporting goods
- The benefits and costs of mass marketing
- The role of advertising
- The practice of smart shopping
- The government's role in consumer protection
- The use of a credit card versus cash

Webbing

PURPOSE

This mental mapping strategy encourages students to think critically as they explore the relationships among events, ideas, and people in a reading passage, lesson, or unit. It may also be used as an assessment tool at the end of a section, chapter, or unit.

IMPLEMENTATION

1. Direct students to begin by identifying the main idea, event, or individual of a set reading passage.

2. Then provide students with copies of the diagram on page 31. Have students enter the main idea, event, or individual in the center circle of the diagram.

3. In the outer circles, have students enter information that is connected or related to the main idea, event, or individual. For example, you might ask students to read Section 1 of Chapter 19 and to web the information on the types of money used in the United States. After entering *Types of Money* in the center circle, students then might add information on the advantages of coins, checks and debit cards, and credit. The web might look like the following example.

4. Have students share and compare their completed webs. Encourage students to explain why they included particular facts about types of money.

After studying Money and Credit, the students' webs might look like this:

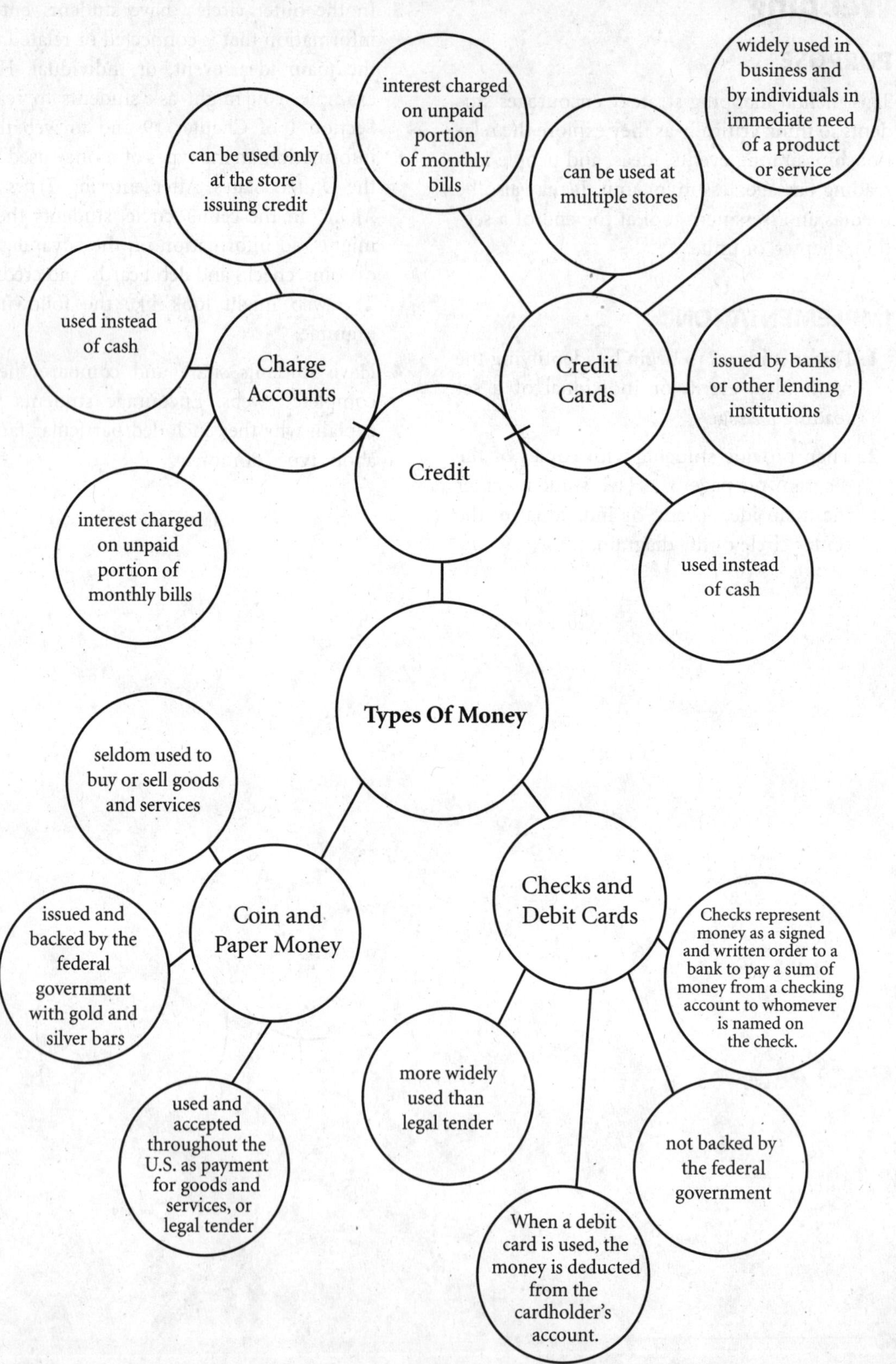

CHAPTER 19   **Personal Finances**

Use this web as a starting point. Then, add or remove circles and lines as necessary.

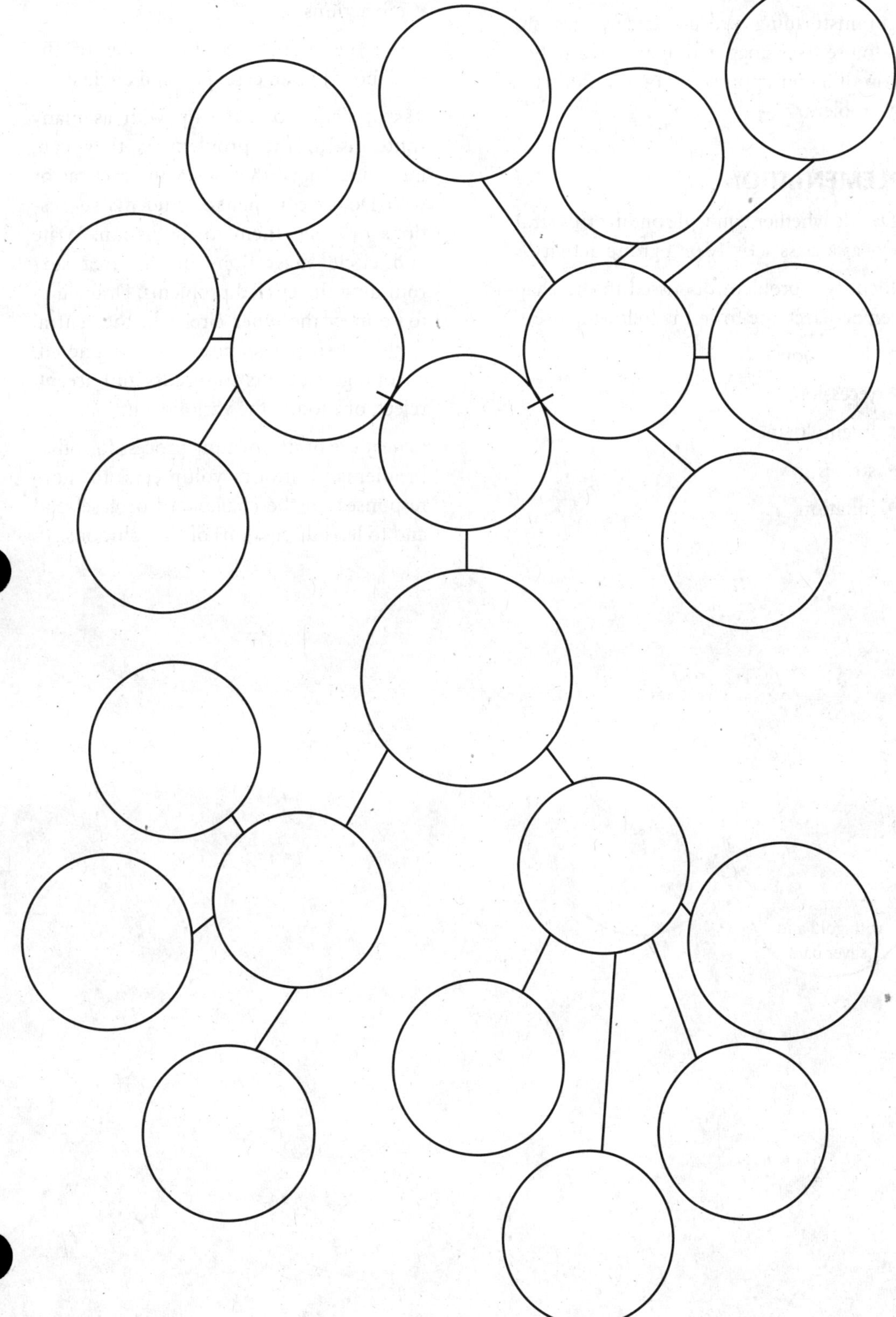

Brainstorming

PURPOSE

The brainstorming process encourages students to use their imagination and creativity to develop different approaches or solutions to a given problem.

IMPLEMENTATION

1. Decide whether you will conduct this strategy as a class activity or a group activity.

2. Identify a problem discussed in the chapter, or select one from the following list:
   - depression
   - recession
   - unemployment
   - strikes
   - inflation
   - lockouts
   - poor working conditions
   - job actions

3. Write the problem in the center of the chalkboard or an easel pad and circle it.

4. Ask students to come up with as many solutions to the problem as they can, including those that seem impractical or wild. Do not comment on students' suggestions or open them to discussion. Write and circle suggestions in the area surrounding the circled problems. Draw lines to connect the outer circles to the central circle. When all responses have been noted, encourage students to discuss and accept, reject, or modify the various solutions.

5. Repeat the brainstorming process for other problems. Call on volunteers to note responses on the chalkboard or easel pad and to lead discussions of the solutions.

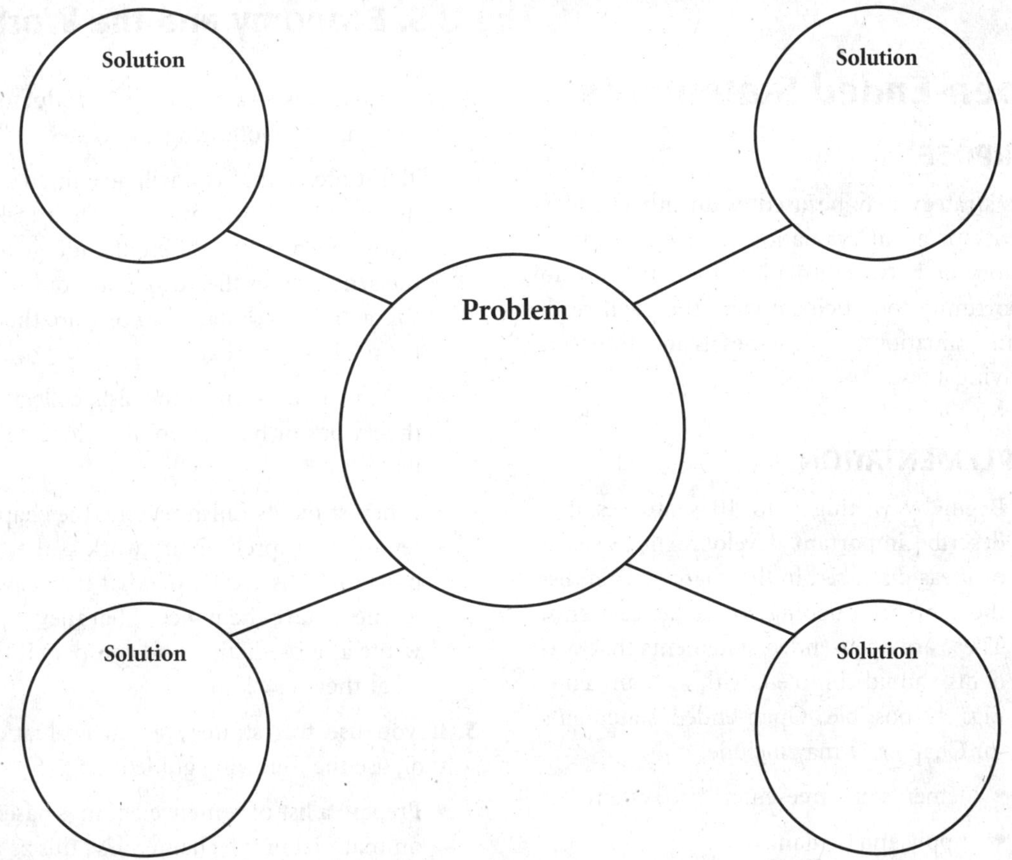
Solution
Solution
Problem
Solution
Solution

Open-Ended Statements

PURPOSE

This strategy may be used as an introductory activity or as an evaluation tool. As an introductory activity, it provides students with an opportunity to anticipate what they will read. As an evaluation tool, it serves as an alternative to giving a test.

IMPLEMENTATION

1. Begin by writing 8 to 10 sentences that describe important developments, events, or ideas discussed in the chapter. Then list the sentence openings or sentence stems. These are open-ended statements that students should complete with as many endings as possible. Open-ended statements for Chapter 21 may include:

   - Elements of a free-enterprise system
   - Supply and demand
   - Ways to invest money
   - Changes in the business cycle
   - The use of economic indicators
   - The influence of current events on the economy
   - The goals of government regulation
   - The relationship between fiscal and monetary policy
   - The impact of international trade
   - The problems of interdependence

2. If you use this strategy as an introductory activity, use the following guidelines:

   - Tell students that you will give them a list of unfinished sentences. Their task is to write as many different endings to the sentences as they can. Point out that this activity is designed to prepare them for reading this chapter.

   - When students finish the task, collect their work or have them file it for later use.

   - When students finish reading the chapter, use their preliminary work as the basis for a discussion of what they have learned. Have them view what they wrote as a prediction and compare it to what they now know.

3. If you use this strategy as an evaluation tool, use the following guidelines:

   - Prepare a list of sentence endings based on material in the chapter. Use this as a measure of students' understanding of the chapter.

   - List the sentence stems on the chalkboard and tell students to complete each sentence in as many ways as the chapter content provides endings.

   - Have students skim the chapter to find the appropriate information or have them write from memory.

   - Encourage students to share and compare their completed sentences.

Ranking

PURPOSE

This strategy gives students practice in choosing among possible alternatives and in openly defending their choices.

IMPLEMENTATION

1. Decide if you want to undertake this strategy as a class or group activity.

2. Begin by directing students to view the seven questions that job seekers should ask themselves when considering a future career, which are listed on textbook pages 560–61.

3. Ask students to suggest which questions they consider the most important. As students respond, ask them to explain and justify their choices.

4. Inform students that they are going to vote by a show of hands for one of the seven questions they think is the most important. Read out each question and have students cast their votes. Keep a tally of the votes and write the results on the board.

5. Next, introduce the idea of weighted tallies. Have students select what they consider are the three most important of the seven questions job seekers should ask themselves. Encourage students to explain their selections. Keep score of first, second, and third place votes on a tally sheet similar to the one on the next page. (If you undertake this strategy as a group activity, make a copy of the tally sheet for each group.)

6. Tally the weighted responses by totaling the first, second, and third place votes for each question. Multiply the votes for first place by three, second place by two, and third place by one. Add up the scores for each question and list the questions on the board in rank order from top to bottom. Place the question with the highest score at the top of the list.

7. Have students compare the weighted ranking with the original ranking.

TALLY SHEET (Example)

Questions to Ask Yourself	1st	2nd	3rd	Total
1. What kind of work will I do in this job?	5	3	1	22
2. What personal qualities does the job require?	0	0	1	1
3. How much education and training does the job require?	3	3	1	16
4. What are the job opportunities in this field?	3	1	2	13
5. How much does the job pay?	4	4	1	21
6. How do I feel about this job?	2	1	0	8
7. Where will I have to live and work for this kind of job?	0	2	3	7

CHAPTER 22   Career Choices

<table>
<tr><th colspan="5">TALLY SHEET</th></tr>
<tr><th>Questions to Ask Yourself</th><th>1st</th><th>2nd</th><th>3rd</th><th>Total</th></tr>
<tr><td>1. What kind of work will I do in this job?</td><td>(__ x 3)</td><td>(__ x 2)</td><td>(__ x 1)</td><td>______</td></tr>
<tr><td>2. What personal qualities does the job require?</td><td>(__ x 3)</td><td>(__ x 2)</td><td>(__ x 1)</td><td>______</td></tr>
<tr><td>3. How much education and training does the job require?</td><td>(__ x 3)</td><td>(__ x 2)</td><td>(__ x 1)</td><td>______</td></tr>
<tr><td>4. What are the job opportunities in this field?</td><td>(__ x 3)</td><td>(__ x 2)</td><td>(__ x 1)</td><td>______</td></tr>
<tr><td>5. How much does the job pay?</td><td>(__ x 3)</td><td>(__ x 2)</td><td>(__ x 1)</td><td>______</td></tr>
<tr><td>6. How do I feel about this job?</td><td>(__ x 3)</td><td>(__ x 2)</td><td>(__ x 1)</td><td>______</td></tr>
<tr><td>7. Where will I have to live and work for this kind of job?</td><td>(__ x 3)</td><td>(__ x 2)</td><td>(__ x 1)</td><td>______</td></tr>
</table>

Predicting Consequences

PURPOSE

This strategy builds on students' understanding of the brainstorming process. It helps students see that the selection of a particular course of action will lead to a predictable set of consequences.

IMPLEMENTATION

1. Begin by presenting students with an issue related to the chapter content—competing in the global economy, for example. Write the issue at the top of the chalkboard.

2. Ask students to brainstorm a number of alternative courses of action to resolve the issue. Then have students select the three most practical suggestions. List these on the chalkboard as the headings of three columns.

3. Have students discuss the alternatives, one by one. Encourage them to think of consequences that might result from taking each course of action. List these consequences on the chalkboard under the appropriate alternative.

4. Ask students which of these consequences they think are negative and which they think are positive, and to what degree. Then have them select what they think is the most appropriate course of action based on the positive and negative consequences.

5. Quickly review the process to demonstrate how considering and predicting consequences can help them choose the best course of action.

6. Organize students into several groups and have them use the predicting consequences process on other issues addressed in Chapter 23. Suggest that they record their work in a graphic organizer similar to the one below. Point out that they may have to adapt the graphic organizer for some issues. For example, they may be able to think of just two alternatives. Encourage groups to present and discuss their issues and preferred courses of action.

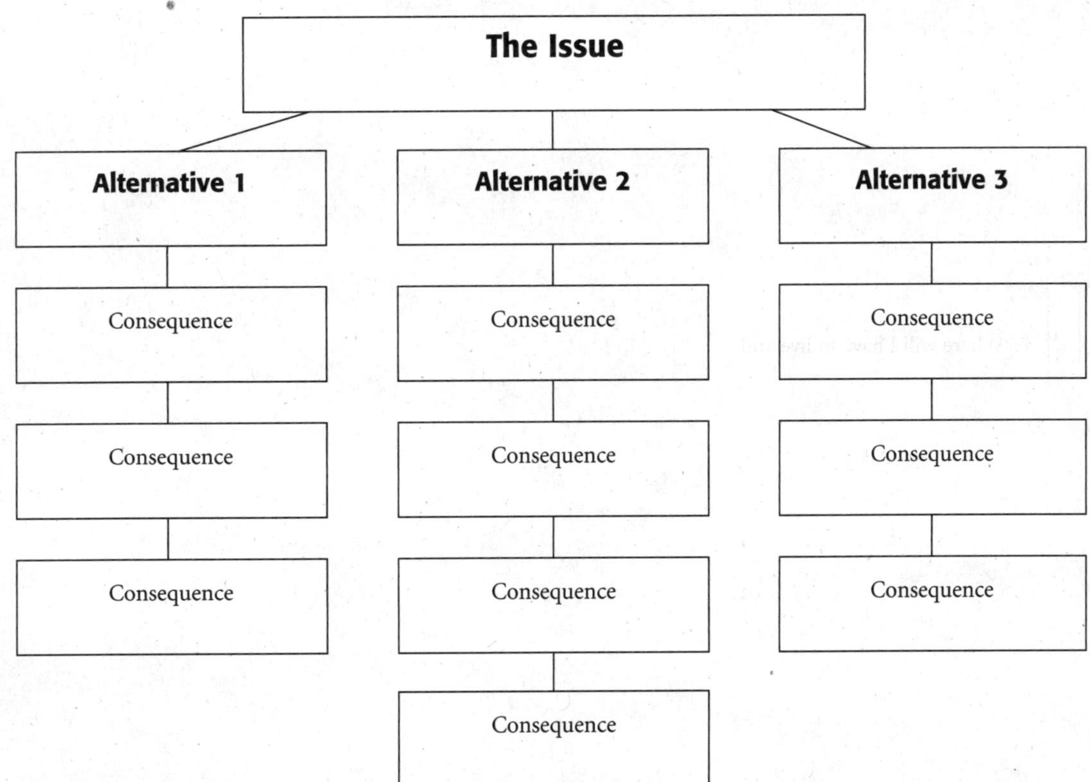

Issue Strip

PURPOSE

The issue strip strategy allows students to create a cartoon strip to represent information that will help them to make a decision on an issue.

IMPLEMENTATION

1. Begin by informing students that for this activity they will create a cartoon strip related to an issue discussed in the chapter.

2. Provide students with copies of the issue strip on the next page. Review the strip with students and have them note that it consists of six equal-sized frames labeled "Created by," "Facts," "Issue," "For," "Against," and "My Decision and Reason." Tell students that their task is to illustrate each frame in the strip to express their knowledge of and feelings about a particular issue.

3. Point out that students should use a combination of appropriate words and pictures to convey their ideas. Add that they may draw their own illustrations or use pictures clipped from magazines and newspapers. Stress that creativity is essential to this activity.

4. Identify and assign issues discussed in the chapter, or make selections from the following list:

   - isolationism
   - the War of 1812
   - the Monroe Doctrine
   - the Good Neighbor Policy
   - the spread of communism
   - the Cold War
   - containment policy
   - the fall of communism
   - the Korean War
   - September 11, 2001 attacks

5. When students have completed the activity, call on volunteers to present and discuss their issue strips.

CHAPTER 24   **Charting a Course**

Created by	Facts	Issue
For	**Against**	**My Decision and Reason**